How Do Things Move?

Pushing and Pulling

Sue Barraclough

www.heinemann.co.uk/library
Visit our website to find out more information about **Heinemann Library** books.

To order:
☎ Phone 44 (0) 1865 888066
▤ Send a fax to 44 (0) 1865 314091
▱ Visit the Heinemann Bookshop at www.heinemann.co.uk/library to browse our catalogue and order online.

First published in Great Britain by Heinemann Library, Halley Court, Jordan Hill, Oxford OX2 8EJ, part of Harcourt Education. Heinemann is a registered trademark of Harcourt Education Ltd.

Editorial: Dan Nunn and Stig Vatland
Design: Jo Hinton-Malivoire and Bigtop
Picture Research: Ruth Blair, Erica Newbery and Kay Altwegg
Production: Duncan Gilbert

Originated by Chroma Graphics (Overseas) Pte. Ltd
Printed and bound in China by South China Printing Company

10 digit ISBN 0 431 02423 5
13 digit ISBN 978 0 431 02423 3

10 09 08 07 06
10 9 8 7 6 5 4 3 2 1

British Library Cataloguing in Publication Data
Barraclough, Sue
Pushing and pulling. - (How do things move?)
1.Energy transfer - Juvenile literature
I.Title
531
A full catalogue record for this book is available from the British Library.

Acknowledgements
The publishers would like to thank the following for permission to reproduce photographs:
Alamy pp. **10, 23 bottom right** (Index Stock), **11, 23 top left** (A Room with Views), **12** (Iain Davidson Photographic), **15, 23 bottom left** (Sarkis Images); Corbis pp. **4, 5**; Corbis pp. **8, 9** (Ed Bock), **13, 22 top left** (LWA-Dann Tardif), **16, 17** (John Henley); Getty Images p. **7**; Getty Images pp. **6, 22 bottom** (Reportage/Per-Anders Pettersson), **18, 19, 23 top right** (Photonica), **21, 22 top right** (photodisc); Harcourt Education pp. **14, 20** (Tudor Photography).

Cover photograph reproduced with permission of Getty (Peter Cade).

Every effort has been made to contact copyright holders of any material reproduced in this book. Any omissions will be rectified in subsequent printings if notice is given to the publishers.

The paper used to print this book comes from sustainable resources.

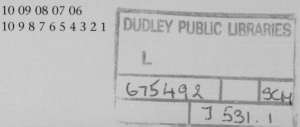

Contents

Pushing and pulling

push

You can push things to make them move.

pull

You can pull
things to make
them move.

Pushing

A push can make a toy car move.

A hard push can make
something move faster.

Pulling

You pull a cart to move it.

Why is this cart hard to pull?

Swinging and spinning

A *push* can make a
swing move higher.

A **push** can make a roundabout spin round.

Moving up

You push yourself up on a seesaw.

You pull yourself up
on a climbing frame.

Moving along

Is this girl pushing
or pulling?

Is this boy pushing
or pulling?

Tug of war

Each team is **pulling** hard on the rope.

Which team do you
think is pulling harder?

Arm wrestling

Both children are *pushing* hard.

Who do you think
is pushing harder?

Light and heavy

The toy car is light.
Is it hard to *push*?

The cart is heavy.
Is it hard to **pull**?

Push or pull?

Can you remember which things you **push** and which things you **pull** ?

Index

Notes for adults

The *How Do Things Move?* series provides young children with a first opportunity to learn about motion. Each book encourages children to notice and ask questions about the types of movement they see around them. The following Early Learning Goals are relevant to the series:

Knowledge and understanding of the world
• Find out about and identify some features of living things and objects
• Ask questions about why things happen and how things work
• Show an interest in the world in which they live
• Encourage use of evaluative and comparative language

These books will also help children extend their vocabulary, as they will hear some new words. Since words are used in context in the book this should enable young children to gradually incorporate them into their own vocabulary.

Follow-up activities
• Show your child two inanimate objects, one heavy and one light. Ask them to decide which item would be easier to push, then get them to test their theory by pushing both objects.
• Attach a toy car to a piece of string and then pull it along at first slowly and then fast. Ask your child if they can identify what made the car move slowly and what made it move fast. Then get them to try for themselves.